Youth LACROSSE UNLEASHED

A Parent's and Player's Guide to the Fundamentals of the Game

The Drummond
Publishing Group

Copyright © 2005
The Drummond Publishing Group

For more information, please contact
The Drummond Publishing Group
362 North Bedford St.
East Bridgewater, MA 02333

Special thanks to ProShots Athletic Center in Pembroke, Massachusetts for hosting our photo shoot. For more information, visit ProShotsCenter.com or call 781-829-9997.

Lacrosse equipment provided by Brine, Inc. of Milford, Massachusetts. For more information, visit Brine.com or call 508-478-3250.

The publisher is not responsible for any injuries sustained while playing lacrosse, practicing the skills described herein, or performing the exercises suggested in this book.

Printed in the United States

ISBN 1-59763-010-1

Library of Congress Control Number: 2005902055

Photography by Suzanne Domenici Walker Photography

CONTENTS

HISTORY

Lacrosse is the oldest sport in North America. Many of the Native American tribes of Canada and the United States played the game. For them, lacrosse was much more than a sport. Native Americans often played *baggataway,* as some called it, to settle disputes between tribes. In this way the game was an alternative to war, and the physical competition was considered excellent training for battle. Some three-day matches pitted teams of 1,000 players playing on fields fifteen miles long!

The name lacrosse is from the stick that every player uses in the game. The sticks the Native Americans used were made of wood and had leather netting woven into the curved top, which formed a pocket used for catching, carrying, and throwing the ball. French missionaries traveling in North America during the 1600s thought these sticks looked like the ceremonial staffs that French bishops carried. These were called *crosses,* or *la crosse.* The name stuck, and baggataway became more widely known as lacrosse.

As early as the 1840s, organized lacrosse leagues had sprung up in eastern Canada. The sport's popularity grew quickly, and today lacrosse is enjoyed throughout the world. Youth lacrosse for boys and girls is growing at one of the fastest rates of any sport in the United States, where membership in youth programs, ages 15 and younger, is now well over 125,000.

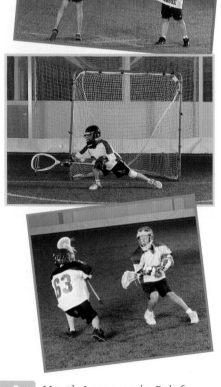

Youth Lacrosse in Brief

Lacrosse is a fast-paced game that combines elements from soccer, football, basketball, and hockey into a unique and fun-to-play sport. Teamwork is an essential part of the game, and at all levels of the sport, the most successful teams are the ones that work well together.

Boys' teams play with 10 players on the field at a time and girls' teams with 12, though beginners often play with fewer. Some players stay on offense and play mostly near their opponent's goal. Other players stay on defense and generally play near their own goal. No matter the position, players can find themselves on any part of the field at any given time, so no position is any more important than another.

Each player carries a stick called a crosse. The crosse has a netted pocket at its top end used for carrying, passing, catching, and shooting the ball. Players use their sticks to move a hard rubber ball about the size of a baseball up the field. They score by shooting the ball into their opponent's goal. Players can either run with the ball or pass it through the air to their teammates. Players defend their goal by trying to intercept a pass, or by scooping up a loose ball on the field with their sticks. Strong stick handling skills are a must for any player, but proper footwork, quick thinking, and the ability to work well with one's teammates are also important skills.

This book will teach you the basic skills you need to play on a lacrosse team. You'll learn about the safety equipment that's needed to protect players from injury. You'll also learn important offensive and defensive skills, ball control, and goalkeeping techniques.

Finally, the rules and regulations section will explain how the game is played. You'll understand what you can and can't do on the field, the penalties that are enforced for breaking the rules, and what the officials' signals mean.

The most important part of lacrosse is having fun. If you develop a love for the game at a young age, the sport will reward you with years of fun, exercise, and excitement. All you need to begin playing lacrosse is a stick, a ball, and a wall—so let's get started!

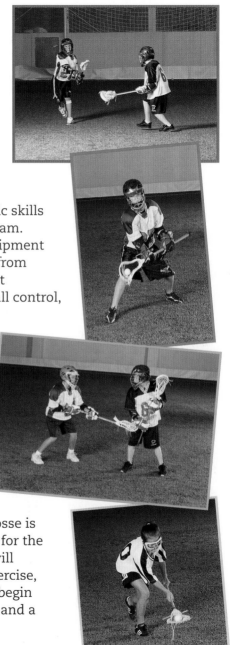

BASIC SKILLS

Warm-Up Exercises

Lacrosse is often called "the fastest game on two feet," and because of its physical demands it's important that you warm up and stretch your muscles before playing. A light jog around the field will help increase your heart rate, and the stretches outlined below will loosen your muscles to help prevent injuries. Stretch slowly and hold the position; don't jerk, rock, or bounce while stretching. You should be able to feel the stretch, but no stretch should ever be painful.

▼ **Spine Twist:** Sitting on the ground, cross your left leg over your right knee. Place both hands on the left side of the body, and turn your head to look over your left shoulder. Reverse to stretch your right side.

▲ **Groin Stretch:** Sitting on the ground with the bottoms of your feet drawn together, use your hands to gently push out and down on your knees.

◀ **Calf Stretch:** Place both hands on a wall or a solid object, like a tree. Bend one knee and place the other leg behind you, keeping your feet facing forward. Press your back heel into the ground.

Back, shoulders, and arms: Standing with your feet shoulder-width apart, put one hand on your hip. Stretch the other arm over your head next to your ear. Bend to one side without leaning forward or backward.

Quadriceps: In a standing position, bring the right foot up to the back of the right thigh. Grasp the foot with your right hand, across the laces of your shoe, and gently pull the foot upward, stretching the large muscle in the front of the thigh.

Hamstring stretch: Sitting on the ground, put one leg straight out in front of you. Bend the other leg to place your foot next to your knee. Keep your back straight as you stretch down from the hips toward your outstretched foot.

Warm-Up Exercises

Before learning about positions and tactics on the field, players must develop the fundamental stick skills needed to pass, catch, shoot, cradle, and scoop the ball. Even the best lacrosse players in the world had to learn and master these basic skills before they learned to do anything else. You can't practice these skills enough! Use the following instructions and illustrations to get a general understanding of each skill, then start practicing. Soon, you'll notice remarkable improvement in your abilities and you'll start to enjoy playing lacrosse more and more. We'll start with how to hold your stick.

Carrying the Stick

Gripping and holding the stick correctly are necessary if a player is to learn the proper techniques of stick handling.

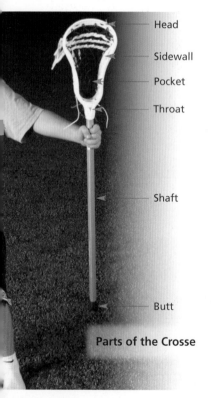

Head

Sidewall

Pocket

Throat

Shaft

Butt

Parts of the Crosse

Start by placing your weak hand (the left hand for right-handed players and the right hand for left-handed players), palm facing your body, about six inches up from the butt of the stick. Place your other hand, known as your strong hand, near the top of the shaft. Hold the stick in a near-vertical position so that the head of the stick is just above your shoulder. Lacrosse coaches will often refer to an imaginary box near your head and shoulder. Becoming comfortable with the stick in this box is important, as you will pass, catch, and cradle the ball with your stick in this position as often as possible.

The "Box"

Cradling

Cradling is one of the more difficult skills to learn. Cradling helps to keep the ball lodged in the pocket of the stick while a player runs down the field past defenders. The cradling motion is similar to rocking or rolling the stick back and forth. This motion creates a gravitational force that prevents the ball from being dislodged from the pocket. Here's how it is done.

Start by holding the stick in a vertical position, with the head in the imaginary box. The top arm and wrist coordinate to roll the stick back and forth in a single, smooth motion.

You may need to watch the ball at first, but eventually learn to cradle without looking at the ball so you can focus your attention down the field.

The next skills you're going to learn—catching, passing, and shooting—can be practiced either with a partner or by yourself, by using an outdoor wall.

Passing

Passing moves the ball from player to player. It allows teams to push the ball up and down the field much faster than any one player could run with it.

The passing motion is much like the overhead motion used to throw a ball. Start by bringing the stick back on the strong side of your body (the same side that your strong hand is on), with your top arm bent fully at the elbow. Your front foot and the elbow of your bottom arm should be pointed at your target.

▶ As you bring the stick forward, your top hand launches upward and forward as it would if you were throwing the ball with your hand. Simultaneously, your bottom hand should pull upwards and back towards your armpit. The timing and coordination of the movements of each arm are important. You'll develop a feel for the correct timing as you practice, and soon it will be automatic.

A Passing Drill

Players pair off and pass a ball back and forth, concentrating on correct form. Coaches can add an element of competition by seeing who can make the most consecutive successful passes and catches, or the most within thirty seconds.

▼ Follow through by snapping your top wrist downwards. This snap provides much of the power behind the pass.

Tip!

Practice passing with only your top hand on the stick. Once this feels comfortable, add the bottom hand.

Catching

Catching a pass uses similar techniques to those used for cradling. The ideal place to catch a pass is with your stick in the box area between your shoulder and head. Not every pass will be on target, though, so you'll need to learn to catch passes in many different positions. Practice these fundamentals.

- Hold the stick so that the pocket is open towards the direction of the pass. The stick should be vertical to the ground, head in the box, to offer the best target.

- Keep your top hand up at the throat of the stick. This makes it much easier to maintain good hand-eye coordination— essential for catching a thrown ball—than if your top hand is lower down.

- Extend the head of the stick slightly forward as the ball approaches. This allows you to provide more "give" as the ball hits the pocket.

- Watch the ball into the widest part of the pocket. As the ball touches the pocket, bend your wrists and pull back on your top hand to provide a soft landing for the ball.

- Secure the ball by moving immediately into the cradling motion.

Be Ready for Anything!

Passes won't always be thrown up near your head, where they're easier to catch. You have to learn to be quick with your hands and feet, so you can adjust to a ball approaching from any angle.

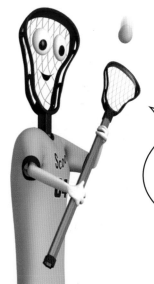

As you're catching the ball, imagine it's an egg that you need to catch without breaking. This will give you an exaggerated sense of how to catch the ball softly.

Shooting

Shooting uses a motion that is similar to passing, though done with more force. The most basic shot is the overhand shot, which is somewhat similar to an overhand throw. Once you master the overhand shot you can develop more creative shots. Advanced players can shoot with an underhand, sidearm, and even behind-the-head ("backhand") motion.

Overhand Shot

▲ With the front shoulder pointed at the target, the arms are flexed, knees bent, weight on the back foot. The stick is brought to an almost horizontal position at shoulder height.

▲ The top hand slides down the stick a few inches to increase power, compared to a pass. As the head of the stick swings up, the back shoulder comes through, weight shifts to the front foot, and the body turns toward the target as the ball is released.

▲ The top arm is fully extended and hips squared to the target on the follow-through.

Keys to Sharp Shooting

- Shots at the corners of the goal are the hardest to defend, so you'll want to develop excellent accuracy with your shots.

- Practice shooting on the run and standing still.

- Your top hand is the main power generator for shooting.

- Good shooting uses the legs and torso as well as the wrists, arms, and shoulders.

- At the end of the follow-through, the head of the stick should be pointing right at the intended target.

- The most powerful shot comes when the ball's final position is near the top of the head of the stick, not in the middle of the pocket.

A Two-Person Shooting Drill

One person moves around behind the goal feeding passes to the shooter from various angles. The shooter tries to quickly catch, cradle, and fire. The shooter can take passes standing still and while running. Switch partners.

Scooping

A lacrosse ball on the ground is up for grabs. Players from both teams will race for the ball, but the first player to scoop the ball into his or her stick will win possession.

The Basic Scooping Position

Bend at your knees and waist. Point your stick downwards so the head is close to the ground. The top hand should be near the throat of the shaft for extra control of the head. The butt end is off to your side—you don't want to jab yourself! Get your back hand down.

Scooping on the Run

Approach the ball directly, sliding the stick along the ground beneath the ball until it rolls up into the pocket. Always run through the ball.

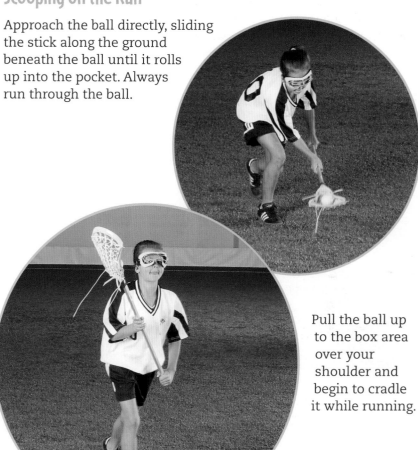

Pull the ball up to the box area over your shoulder and begin to cradle it while running.

Dodging

Dodging means carrying the ball and getting around defenders, by using various tactics. The best offensive players learn to combine fakes, bursts of speed, sudden twists and turns—whatever works. You can use dodges to fool your opponent about where you're going.

The Face Dodge

In this dodge, you cross your stick in front of your face to move around a defender or keep the defender off balance.

◁ As you're running towards a defender, your stick is to one side of your body.

◁ Move your stick to the other side of your body by passing it in front of your face.

▽ Keep your head up and eyes downfield.

Tip!

After passing the defender, return your stick to its original position.

The Split Dodge

The split dodge is a good open-field move to get away from a defender who is running alongside you, hip-to-hip.

▶ Start by getting the defender on your hip, with your body between him and your stick.

▶ Plant your stick-side foot and push off in the opposite direction. Quickly bring your stick across your face. Switch hands and put the head of the stick up in the box on the other side.

▶ Sprint away before the defender can recover.

The Roll Dodge

The roll dodge is used to get around a defender who is standing in front of you as you approach on the run.

▶ For a left-handed player, start the dodge by running at a defender. Plant your right foot near the defender and pull your stick back. (If you're right-handed, simply reverse the hand and foot instructions and use the same techniques.)

◀ Pivot on the right foot away from the defender. Spin around the defender by pulling your body by the stick. You can switch hands depending on what direction you head off in.

◀ Your back will protect the ball as you bring your right foot around the defender.

As you become more comfortable moving with the ball in your crosse, you'll be able to invent your own dodges and really surprise the defense. The key is to sprint—that's the best way to defeat a defender!

Scoop
04

Marking

Marking is how a defender guards an offensive player without the ball. The defender wants to try to prevent him or her from receiving a pass and scoring. Effective marking is the foundation of a good defense.

Keys to Marking

- The ideal position for marking is to have one foot behind and the other alongside the player you're guarding. From this position you can quickly move in front of your opponent to steal a pass.

- In girls' lacrosse, a defender may not be within the 8-meter arc for more than three seconds unless she is closely marking an opponent.

- Defenders need to develop good "field vision" and be able to watch both the opponent they are marking and the player with the ball.

- A stick's length is about as far away as you'll ever want to be from the player you're guarding.

- Generally mark an opponent in the midfield by being between him or her and the goal. In the immediate goal area defenders may need to mark by getting in front of opponents and turning their back to the ball.

- Keep your stick in the up and ready position.

- Off-the-ball defenders generally play with their backs to the goal.

- Always know where the ball is and where the person you're defending is.

Body Checking

A "body check" means somewhat different things in boys' and girls' lacrosse. Girls' lacrosse is not a contact sport. It's illegal for the defender to touch the player with the ball. Players are not allowed to charge or barge, or to shoulder or back into, an opponent. Defenders cannot push with the hands or body, nor detain an opponent by holding or pushing with the body or the crosse.

Thus, in girls' lacrosse, a defensive player does a body check by positioning herself between the offensive player with the ball and the goal. By following or mirroring her opponent's every move, the defender tries to slow her opponent down or force her to pass the ball or to move away from the goal.

In boys' lacrosse, youth leagues for ages 11 and younger generally also prohibit body-to-body contact.

Lacrosse for older boys is a contact sport, however, and a "body check" is more physical. Under certain conditions defensive players can use the body to physically block an opponent. All contact must occur from the front or side, and be above the waist and below the neck.

Tips for Guarding an Opponent

- Maintain your balance so you're ready to move in any direction at any time.

- Keep your eyes on the ball and try to mirror the stick movements of your opponent.

- Always stay in front of your opponent, and try to block his or her line of vision down the field.

- Run with the opponent and try to cut off his or her path to the goal, much as you guard someone with the ball in a game of basketball.

Boys' Body Checking: What You Can't Do

In boys' lacrosse, it is against the rules to do various types of body checks. You can't:

- body check an opponent who is not in possession of the ball or within five yards of a loose ball
- body check an opponent after he has passed or shot the ball
- apply a body check during which you take one or both hands off of your crosse
- initiate a body check with your helmet
- do "take-out" checks—hard-hitting checks where a player hits with the shoulders in an effort to knock the ball-carrier onto the ground

Stick Checking

Stick checking is using your stick to knock the ball out of your opponent's stick. The stick check should be a controlled and compact chopping or poking movement. You will be penalized if you swing your stick wildly and dangerously at another player. You will also be penalized if you hit a part of your opponent's body other than their gloved hand (considered part of the stick in lacrosse) with your stick.

As with body checks, youth leagues may limit what's allowed. In general boys can stick check from the front, back, or side, while the girls' game is more restricted.

Stick Checking Rules for Girls' Lacrosse

In recent years girls' youth leagues have begun to adopt a "no stick-checking" policy for players up to the sixth-grade level. The thinking is that developing players should concentrate on proper techniques for cradling, passing, and so forth, and that stick checking interferes with these skills.

For girls in the seventh and eighth grade, some programs are adopting a "modified stick-checking" policy. This means that the defensive player is allowed to check an opponent's stick if it is below shoulder level, and only by using a downward motion away from the other player's body. A check should never be allowed near a player's head or face.

Tip!

In girls' lacrosse, a player with the ball in her crosse may not protect it by cradling so close to her body or face so as to make a legal, safe check impossible for the opponent.

Scoop

04

In women's lacrosse, stick checking can be done only when a defender is one step in front of her opponent. It is not legal to reach across an opponent's body to check the handle of a crosse when the defender is even with or behind that opponent. Because women don't wear helmets, stick checks must be directed away from an imaginary 7-inch sphere or "bubble" around the head of the player.

Poke Check

The defender pokes with the head of the stick at the offensive player's bottom hand on the stick. The movement should be a short, quick, poking action.

A Guarding Drill

Set two cones on the midfield line, 5 feet apart. One player runs with the ball from the goal line towards midfield. Another player must mark the player with the ball and perform body checks to prevent him or her from running across the midfield line between the two cones. For boys, the defender can also try to poke check the bottom hand while staying upfield of the dodger. Players should alternate between offense and defense.

Face-Offs

A face-off at the center of the field begins each period of play and occurs after each goal. A team that can consistently control the face-off will have a significant advantage over its opponents. The face-off is somewhat different for boys' and girls' games.

Boys

In boys' lacrosse, each face-off player is on the defensive side of the center line. In a crouching position, they hold their sticks along the center line, positioned so that the pockets are back-to-back. Both hands must be on the handle of the stick and touching the ground. There must be just enough space between the pockets of the sticks for the official to place the ball between them. After the ball is placed, the official says "set" and the two players must be motionless until the official blows the whistle.

To perform a face-off:

- Crouch with your feet hip-width apart. Your hands and feet must be to the left of the throat of your stick.
- Hold your right hand palm-up and as close to the throat of the stick as is comfortable.
- Hold your left hand palm-down, anywhere from 8 to 12 inches down from your right hand.
- Some players like to place the right elbow against the inside of the right knee.
- As you crouch near the ground, the wall of the stick should be completely flush with the ground.
- When the whistle blows, go after the ball with your stick and attempt to scoop it up or knock it to a teammate.

Girls

In girls' lacrosse, the players perform the face-off, or draw, from a standing rather than squatting position.

- The pockets of the sticks are put back-to-back, horizontally at approximately waist level. The ball is placed between the pockets.

- When the whistle blows, the players must fling the ball upwards by moving their sticks up and away from each other. The ball must pass above the players' heads for the draw to be legal. After the ball is airborne, the players attempt to catch the ball or knock it to a teammate.

Goalkeeping

The goalie is the team's last line of defense. A good goaltender is the anchor of the defensive team. While in the goal-crease area, the goalie can stop the ball with any part of the body, including the hands—goalies are the only players on the field who can touch the ball with their hands. The traits a goalie should possess include quickness, confidence, and intelligence.

Defending the Goal

- Stand with your feet shoulder-width apart and your weight on the balls of your feet. Keep your back straight and your shoulders back. From this position you'll be ready to move quickly in any direction.

- Hold your stick with your top hand close to the throat of the stick and your bottom hand 8 to 12 inches below. Goalies make most of their saves with the stick. As a shot comes towards you, always step toward the shooter. Your hands and body will naturally follow, moving you into the proper position to make a save.

- Position yourself between the ball and the goal. Always know where the ball is on the field.

- When the ball is behind the net, turn your body to face that direction. As the ball comes around to the front of the net, move to whichever side of the goal the ball is coming from.

This is a good goalie stance, with feet shoulder-width apart, hands not too close.

This stance has both hands and feet too close together.

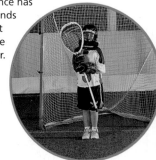

Common Goalie Errors

Beginning goalies often make the same mistakes. If you can avoid these common pitfalls you'll make it harder for the offense to score.

✘ Losing concentration. Just because the ball is at the other end of the field doesn't mean you don't have to pay attention to the game.

✘ Moving backwards into the net. If you move backwards too quickly you're only giving the shooter more open angles to shoot from.

✘ Moving too far out from the net. If you're too far out of the goal, the shooter will be able to run right past you and shoot into the open net.

✘ Losing track of where you are in relation to the net. If you're too far off to one side, shooters will find it easy to shoot the ball into the other side of the goal.

Move in an Arc

Indoor lacrosse fields may have a half-circle in front of the goal rather than the regulation crease. You can use its radius as a guideline for how to move in an arc, rather than simply in a straight line, between the goal posts. This will limit the angles from which an attacker can shoot.

A Goaltending Drill

Face a wall and have a coach or teammate stand behind you. Stand about 10 yards from the wall and have the person behind you throw the ball off of the wall. As the ball bounces back to you, step and react to it as if it were a shot. Gradually move closer to the wall so that you must move faster and faster to stop the ball from getting by you. Have your coach or teammate throw the ball so it bounces back to you at high, mid, and low angles.

Clearing

The goalie is a team's last defender, and can also be the first offensive player. After making a save, the goalie must pass the ball to a teammate. This is called clearing the ball. Passing is a little more difficult with a goalie's stick than it is with an attacker's or defender's stick because the head is oversized. Here are a few pointers for clearing the ball:

⚙ Secure the ball in the stick's pocket with a wide side-to-side cradling motion.

⚙ Exaggerate the wrist motion you would use if passing with a regular stick. This will help you be more accurate with your passes.

⚙ Use an overhand motion to release the ball.

Tip!

To set up a successful clear, one defender splits off toward a sideline to receive the initial pass from the goalie. Meanwhile, another defender releases upfield to get open for a second pass.

Setting Picks

You can help your teammates get free from defenders by setting picks. When you set a pick your body acts as a barrier between a defender and your teammate. A well-placed pick can create open scoring chances for your team and is hard to defend. Here's how to help out your teammates by setting a pick.

Tip!

As an attacker, run very close to any pick set for you. This will make sure that your defender's pursuit is successfully blocked.

- ⭐ You must be standing still when you set a pick—you're not even allowed to lean over to pick a defender. Stand with your feet wide enough apart to provide a solid base.

- ⭐ Note that youth rules may require that any pick be set within a defender's view. The intent is to prevent injuries from a full-speed collision.

- ⭐ Hold your stick in a vertical position, close to your body.

- ⭐ Brace yourself for contact as the defender comes towards you. You'll want the defender to run into a part of your body that is protected by padding, like your chest and shoulders.

- ⭐ After you've set the pick, turn and cut in the opposite direction or towards the goal and be ready to catch a pass. This is the same "pick-and-roll" strategy used in basketball.

RULES AND REGULATIONS

The Field

Both boys' and girls' lacrosse are played on a flat field similar to a soccer or football field. Regulation-size fields are quite large, but youth lacrosse is played on smaller fields that vary by gender and age. See page 35 for the dimensions of some common youth fields.

Boys' Fields

Boys' lacrosse fields are rectangular, with the long edges called the **sidelines** and the short ones **end lines**. The 6-by-6-foot **goals** are on opposite ends of the field, in the middle of circles (with up to a 9-foot radius) called the **crease**. The 6-foot-long line between goal posts is the **goal line**. There can be up to 15 yards of playing area behind each goal. The **center** or **midfield line** extends across the middle of the field, perpendicular to the sidelines. An "X" at the midpoint of this line is the **center**. The field is further divided into three sections roughly equal in size. The **midfield area** extends an equal distance in each direction from the center line. Each team, depending upon which goal they are shooting at, has an **attack area** and a **defensive area**; these are also known as the **goal areas**. Designated **wing areas** run parallel to each sideline within the midfield area. Finally, a **special substitution area** is off the playing field on each side of the center line.

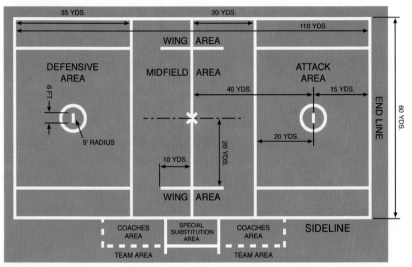

Girls' Fields

Girls' lacrosse fields are the same general size and shape as boys' fields, although girls' fields do not have measured boundaries. Rather, officials designate "visible guidelines" to indicate agreed-upon boundaries before each the game. A **center circle** midway between the two goals is where the draws are held. A horizontal line in front of each goal (which are the same size as the boys') is called the **restraining line** (it is about 30 yards in front of the goal on a 100-yard-long field). Only 7 offensive players and 8 defensive players (including the goalie) are allowed beyond the restraining line at a time. Additionally, there is an **8-meter arc** in front of both goals and a larger semi-circle called the **12-meter fan**, which play a role in positioning and penalties. A circle around the goal marks the **goal circle**, which may be entered only by the goalie or the deputy.

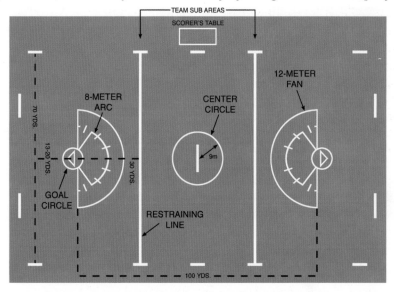

Recommended Field Sizes for Boys' and Girls' Lacrosse

	Boys		Girls	
Age	Field Size	Behind Goal	Field Size	Behind Goal
9 and under	60 x 40 yards	5 yards	70 x 25 yards	10 yards
9 and 10	90 x 50 yards	10 yards	110 x 50 yards	10 yards
11 and over	110 x 60 yards	15 yards	120 x 70 yards	10 yards

Equipment

Lacrosse is a fast-paced game played with a stick and a hard ball, and for these reasons a fair amount of equipment is needed to keep players from getting hurt. Lacrosse equipment can range widely in price, but beginners can get started at a low cost. Here's what you'll need.

Uniforms

Lacrosse players wear lightweight athletic jerseys, usually made of mesh. Some leagues may require girls to wear skirts, while others allow shorts. Boys play in shorts.

The Crosse

The stick carried by all players on the field is called a crosse. The crosse is a very important piece of equipment. Used for moving the ball up and down the field, players must become as comfortable with the crosse as they are with their own hands. The handle is usually made of wood or aluminum, and the head plastic. The mesh or net that forms the pocket is nylon, often with some leather strings.

Crosse sizes vary by position and differ somewhat for boys' and girls' leagues. There are minimum and maximum requirements for the length of the crosse, as well as for the width of the head. Except for some beginning leagues, the depth of the pocket cannot be greater than the diameter of the ball (see page 37). Refer to the table below to find the correct crosse sizes for your position. Keep in mind that younger players will want to use smaller sticks than those the more experienced players use.

Crosse Size Requirements for Boys' and Girls' Lacrosse

| Position | Boys | | Girls | |
	Length	Head Width	Length	Head Width
Offense	37–40"	6.5–10"	35.5–43.25"	7–10"
Defense	37–72"	6.5–10"	35.5–43.25"	7–10"
Goalkeeper	37–72"	10–12"	35.5–48"	10–12"

No matter what position you play, it's important that you use a crosse size that is comfortable for you. In lacrosse, the crosse acts as your hands, so the more comfortable you are with your stick, the more success you'll have on the field.

No Deep Pockets Allowed

The crosse is designed to create a balance between offense and defense. If the netting in the head of the stick were allowed to be loose, offensive players would be able to hold onto the ball quite easily. Defenders would have a hard time jarring the ball out of the deep pocket. The rules promote skillful cradling by limiting the depth of the net.

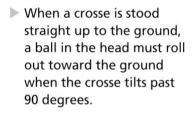

▶ When a crosse is stood straight up to the ground, a ball in the head must roll out toward the ground when the crosse tilts past 90 degrees.

▽ As the head of the crosse is rotated forward from 90 degrees the ball should roll over the sidewall toward the ground.

90°

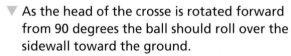

▽ If you can see light between the top of the ball and bottom edge of the sidewall, this is an illegal deep pocket. Note that in some beginning youth lacrosse leagues, this rule is relaxed to allow a "modified deep pocket"—the ball may be up to half-a-ball below the sidewall.

The Ball

The official lacrosse ball is made of hard rubber. It can be white, yellow, or orange, is 7.75–8 inches around, and weighs about 5 ounces. Somewhat softer lacrosse balls have been developed for use in beginner's leagues, as well for practice.

Helmets

Lacrosse helmets for boys are complete with a facemask, a chin pad, and a chinstrap. Hard helmets are not allowed in girls' lacrosse, with the exception of the goalie, who must wear one. Soft protective headgear is permitted in girls' lacrosse.

Mouth and Eye Guards

Mouthpieces must be worn by all youth lacrosse players whenever a hard ball is being used. Goggle-like eye guards have recently become mandatory for use in girls' lacrosse.

Gloves

Protective gloves are recommended for players in girls' lacrosse leagues and required for all boys' lacrosse players. Goalies wear larger gloves with extra padding.

Try on some teammates' gloves to get a sense of what model is best for your hands.

Pads

In boys' lacrosse, arm and shoulder pads are required. Rib pads are not required but are strongly recommended for providing extra protection. All forms of padding are optional in girls' lacrosse (again, the goalie is an exception), though some leagues may have special requirements.

Shoes

At the youngest levels, players wear sneakers. Rubber-cleated shoes, like those used for soccer or football, become common at higher levels.

The Goalie's Equipment

The goaltender wears the most equipment on the field. In addition to helmets, gloves, and arm/shoulder pads, male goalies typically wear abdominal padding, a throat guard, leg padding, and an athletic cup. Female goalies are required to wear a hard helmet with a facemask, protective gloves, and throat and chest protectors. Pads on the shins and thighs are highly recommended. All padding used by goalies should be lightweight and fit snugly to allow a free range of movement.

Boys' Positions

Boys' lacrosse is played with 10 players on the field: 3 attackmen, 3 midfielders, 3 defensemen, and the goalie.

Attackmen

Attackmen are the primary goal scorers in lacrosse. They generally play on their opponent's half of the field and work to get open shots on goal. Attackmen should have excellent stick handling skills and neat footwork in order to avoid defenders and maneuver towards the net. Getting open shots on goal requires crisp, accurate passes to move the ball quickly through the offensive zone and draw the defense out of position.

Midfielders

Midfielders are important to both a team's offense and its defense. Midfielders must cover the entire length of the field, so they should have good stamina and speed. The midfielders are the key to the transition game—when possession of the ball changes sides, and the team on offense must now play defense, and vice versa. Midfielders scoop up loose balls, take passes from the goalie after a saved shot, and move the ball from one end of the field to the other. When their team is on defense, the midfielders drop back to defend their goal, and when their team is on offense, the midfielders work with the attackers to try to score.

▶ Typical positions are shown (one team only) for the goalie (G), defensemen (D), midfielders (M), and attackmen (A).

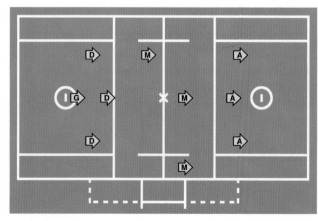

Defensemen

A defenseman's job is to prevent the other team's offense from scoring goals. Defensemen try to keep the ball away from their own net so that the opposing team doesn't get any easy shots on goal. The longer stick a defenseman uses allows him to apply pressure on the attackmen without playing so close that he's easily beaten by a dodge. While marking an attacker the defenseman must apply pressure but not to such an extent that he is unable to recover if beaten. Defenders can stick check attackmen and, in upper divisions, perform legal body-to-body checks. If a defenseman is able to take the ball from his opponent, he should look to get the ball downfield by passing to one of his midfielders.

Goaltenders

Quick on his feet and willing to put his body between the ball and the goal, a good goalie is the leader of the defense. But a goalie should not get too down on himself after letting a ball past him for a goal. Lacrosse is a team effort. Goals are either scored or let in by the collective efforts of the team as a whole, not by one individual.

The goalie should be able to read the opposing offense and instruct his defensemen on where to go and how to react to an offensive attack. The goalie is protected from any kind of checking when he's in the goal crease, but once he comes out he's vulnerable to being checked. After making a save, the goalie positions his team to clear the ball down the field. In upper divisions of play, the goalie has four seconds to pass or run the ball out of the crease after making a save.

Tip!

Beginning youth lacrosse leagues may play games with as few as seven field players and no goalie.

Girls' Positions

Girls' lacrosse is played with 12 players, including the goalie. Of the field players, 5 are mostly on offense, and 6 mostly on defense (the center plays the whole field).

Attackers

The three main attackers in the girls' sport play positions called first, second, and third home, depending on the area of the field they cover.

First Home

The first home plays closest to her opponent's net. She is a major scorer and is constantly looking to get open in front of the net for a shot on goal. First home must be an excellent shooter and passer.

Second Home

Second home plays in the middle of her opponent's half of the field. She works with first home to get open shots on goal. She must be able to shoot from any distance and make accurate passes, or feeds, to first home near the goal.

▼ Typical positions are shown (one team only) for the goalie (G), point (P), coverpoint (CP), third man (TM), left and right defense wings (DW), center (C), left and right attack wings (AW), third home (TH), second home (SH), and first home (FH).

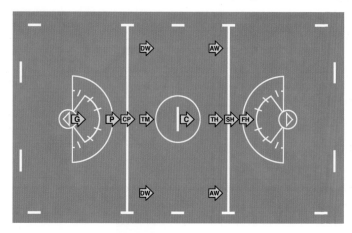

Third Home

The third home is the key player in transitioning the ball from offense to defense and defense to offense. She plays midfield and her responsibilities are similar to those of the midfielder in boys' lacrosse, including moving the ball from the defensive to the offensive zone and posing an offensive threat from the wing areas.

Attack Wings

The left and right attack wings work closely with third home to transition the ball from defense to offense. They provide a scoring threat and should be able to run and pass the ball effectively.

Defenders

Defense Wings

The defense wings mark the left and right attack wings. The left defense wing marks the right attack wing and the right defense wing marks the left attack wing. The defense wings play in the midfield and bring the ball into the attack area.

Center

The center plays both offense and defense. She takes draws and runs all over the field. The center marks the opposing center.

Third Man

The third man marks third home. She plays close to midfield and should be able to pass the ball downfield to her offensive players.

Coverpoint

The coverpoint marks second home. Like the point, she needs to be able to play solid defense against the opponent's second home.

Point

The point marks first home. She is the last defender on her side of the field before the goalie. She should be able to contest her opponent's shot and keep her body between first home and the goal. The point should stand in the goal (as the "deputy") if the goalkeeper runs out of the crease with the ball.

Goalie

The goalie in girls' lacrosse is responsible for the same duties as her counterpart in the boys' game.

Officials

From one to three officials (an umpire, a referee, and a field judge) control the play on the field. Their main job is to:

⊙ Make sure players' equipment is legal.

⊙ Start the game by placing the ball in the middle of the field, saying "set," and blowing the whistle.

⊙ Enforce the rules of play and call penalties, judge when a ball goes out of bounds, and decide when a goal has been scored.

OFFICIAL SIGNALS

▲ **Score**
Both hands raised over the head means score.

▲ **No Score**
Arms down, making a crossing motion, means no score.

▲ **Timeout**
For discretionary or injury timeout, crossing the hands over the head is followed by tapping of the hands on the chest.

▲ **Play On**
Dead ball or dead ball followed by appropriate foul signal.

▲ **Face-off**
Hands at abdomen, palms in, with a sweeping movement outward.

Alternate Possession
The face-off movement, then pointing in the direction of possession.

Ball in Attack Area
Raised right hand points down to attack area.

Out of Bounds/ Direction of Play
Right arm extends and bends up and down at elbow, showing direction of play.

Personal Foul
Right arm raised, index finger extended.

Interference
Arms crossed at chest.

Stalling
Hands grasp forearms at abdomen.

Offside
Hands on hips.

Duration of Play

Lacrosse games are usually divided into four quarters. The table below shows the typical lengths of lacrosse games by age level. There is a two-minute break between the first and second quarters and the third and fourth quarters. The side of the field a team's goal is on changes between quarters. A ten-minute break between the second and third quarters is called halftime. If the teams are tied at the end of four quarters of play, a four-minute overtime period can be played. The first team to score a goal in overtime wins the game. If neither team scores after the first overtime period, additional overtimes are played until a team scores, though some youth leagues will end games in a tie.

Age	Boys Time of Play	Girls
9 and under	48 minutes running time 4 12-minute quarters	40 minutes running time 4 10-minute quarters
10–12	48 minutes running time 4 12-minute quarters	50 minutes running time 4 12:30-minute quarters
13–15	40 minutes stop clock 4 10-minute quarters	50 minutes running time 4 12:30-minute quarters

Note that some youth leagues use a modified running time in which the clock stops when the whistle is blown during the last two minutes of each quarter.

Starting the Game

Before the game starts, the official holds a coin toss with the captains of each team. The winner of the coin toss chooses which end of the field their team will attack in the first quarter.

The game begins with a face-off. A face-off begins play after halftime, and after a goal is scored, too.

Out of Bounds

The official blows his or her whistle when the ball goes out of bounds. In girls' lacrosse, at the sound of the whistle, all players must stop and stand still so the official can decide who was closest to the ball when it went out of bounds. Possession is given to the player who was closest to the ball when and where it went out of bounds.

In boys' lacrosse, when the ball or the player with the ball goes out of bounds, the other team is given possession. When the ball goes out of bounds after a shot, the player closest to the ball where it went out of bounds gets possession.

Scoring

A goal is scored when the whole ball completely crosses the goal line that runs between the goalposts. In addition to throwing the ball into the net, in regulation lacrosse it is legal to kick the ball with your foot (ouch!) or bat it into the net with your stick (though not with your hands). Youth leagues may require scoring to be off a crosse. Each goal is worth one point (professional lacrosse has two-point goals), and the team with the most goals wins. Some beginning leagues may have a three-pass rule, requiring for a goal to count that the offense make at least three passes before shooting.

Offsides

In boys' lacrosse, both teams must have at least four players on their defensive side of the midfield line and at least three players on their offensive side of the midfield line. A team is penalized for offsides if it doesn't have the right amount of players on each side of the field. If a team is offsides while it has the ball, the official stops play and gives the ball to the other team. If the team without the ball is offsides, then one player from the penalized team must serve a 30-second suspension. During the suspension, the team with the ball has an advantage because they have one more player on the field than their opponent does.

Offsides is not enforced in girl's lacrosse. Girls must watch their positioning, however, in relation to the restraining line, which marks an area where only 7 offensive and 8 defensive players can be at a time.

Fouls

Fouls in girls' lacrosse are called either major or minor, while fouls in boys' lacrosse are called either personal or technical.

Girls' Major Fouls

Charging, slashing, blocking, playing in a rough, dangerous, or unsportsmanlike manner, and checking in leagues where checking is not allowed are considered major fouls. The penalty for a major foul is a free position for the team that was fouled. During a free position, all defenders must be at least four meters away from the player being awarded the free position. At the sound of the whistle, the player with the ball may run, pass, or shoot the ball.

Girls' Minor Fouls

Minor fouls occur when a player enters the goal crease, wards off an opposing player with her hands, or checks the stick of a player who doesn't have the ball. A ball hitting a player's body to her advantage is a minor foul. The penalty for minor fouls is an indirect free position. An indirect free position is the same as a free position, except that shooting is not allowed.

Boys' Personal Fouls

The penalty for a personal foul is a one- to three-minute suspension from play for the offending player and possession to the team that was fouled. A player with five personal fouls is ejected from the game. A suspended player remains in the penalty box until he is released by the timekeeper, the opposing team scores a goal, or the penalized team gets possession of the ball in its attack-goal area. Most rough play results in a personal foul, including slashing, tripping, cross checking, illegal body checking, and unnecessary roughness.

Boys' Technical Fouls

Holding, interference, offsides, pushing, and warding off an opponent with one's hands are technical fouls. The penalty for a technical foul is possession of the ball to the team that was fouled or, if the fouled team had possession of the ball at the time of the foul, a player from the offending team must serve a 30-second suspension. The slow whistle is also used for technical fouls when the fouled team has an immediate goal scoring opportunity.

DICTIONARY OF COMMON LACROSSE TERMS

Arc In girls' lacrosse, the wedge-shaped area that extends 8 meters in front of the goal; a defender can remain in the 8-meter arc for only 3 seconds unless she is within a stick's length of an opponent.

Attack Area In boys' lacrosse, the section of the field around the goal the team is shooting at.

Attack Wings In girls' lacrosse, the offensive players who play on each side of the midfield area; attack wings are often speedy players who can help in the transition from defense to offense.

Attackmen In boys' lacrosse, the players positioned in the offensive end of the field, who score most of a team's goals; also known as attackers.

Ball Lacrosse balls are made of hard rubber and are 8 inches in circumference and 5 ounces in weight—slightly smaller than but the same weight as a baseball.

Body Check In boys' lacrosse, using the shoulder to bump a ball carrier, or a player within 5 yards of a loose ball, above the waist and below the neck; in girls' lacrosse, using positioning and mirroring of the offensive player's movements to slow her down or force her in another direction.

Bounce Shot A shot on goal that bounces before the goal line.

Box Lacrosse An indoor version of lacrosse, with walls that define the playing area.

Breakaway A scoring opportunity in which a shooter gets by the defense and closes in for a one-on-one shot against the goalie.

Butt The bottom end of the stick, usually capped with a plastic plug.

Cage Another name for the goal.

Catch Receiving and controlling the ball in the head of the crosse.

Center In girls' lacrosse, the player who plays in the center midfield area; she takes all draws and plays both offense and defense; also, on the field, the spot where draws and face-offs are taken.

Center Line The line across the center of the field of play; also known as the midfield line.

Check Up A call that goalies use to remind defensive players to mark opponents.

Clear Moving the ball from the defense to the offense, such as by passing or carrying the ball out of the defensive half of the field.

Closely Guarded In girls' lacrosse, when a player with the ball has an opponent within a sticks length.

Coverpoint In girls' lacrosse, the defender who plays in the center, second out from her team's goal; she marks the other team's second home.

Cradle Rocking the head of the stick back and forth to keep the ball in the pocket from centrifugal force.

Crease The circular area around the goal, which can be entered only by defensive players; also known as the goal circle.

Critical Scoring Area In girls' lacrosse, an area, including the 8-meter arc and 12-meter fan, in front of, to each side, and behind the goal; fouls by defenders inside this area may result in special penalties.

Cross Check A type of check, not allowed in youth lacrosse, in which a player uses the stick handle between the hands to push an opponent.

Crosse The stick, used to catch, cradle, and carry the ball.

Crosse Check A stick check.

Cut A quick movement to elude a defensive player.

Defense Wings In girls' lacrosse, the two players who play on either side of the center midfield area; they mark attack wings and help transition the ball from defense to offense.

Defensemen In boys' lacrosse, the three players who play nearest the home goal, defending the other team's scorers.

Defensive Area In boys' lacrosse, the section of the field around the goal the team is defending.

Deputy In girls' lacrosse, a defensive player who may only enter or remain in the goal circle when her team is in possession of the ball and the goalkeeper is out of the goal circle.

Dodge Any of a number of movements, such as a split and a roll, that a player with the ball uses to get by a defender.

Dominant Hand The hand of a player's throwing arm, used as the top hand for hard shots.

Draw In girls' lacrosse, the face-off that puts the ball in play at the start of each period and after a goal is scored; the ball is placed between the horizontal sticks of two players standing at the center of the field; they must fling the ball over head height before challenging for possession.

End Lines On the boys' field, the two boundary lines across the field behind the goals.

Extra-Man Offense Scoring plays designed to take advantage of the other team having one or more players in the penalty box; also known as a power play (as in ice hockey) and man-up offense.

Face Dodge An offensive move that involves bringing the stick around the face while cutting past a defender.

Face-Off In boys' lacrosse, placing the ball on the ground between two opposing, squatting players, as a way to put the ball in play at the start of each period and after a goal is scored.

Fan In girls' lacrosse, the semi-circular-shaped area that extends twelve meters in front of the goal; also known as the twelve-meter fan.

Fast Break A quick attack that gives the offense a one (or more) player advantage as they attempt to score.

First Home In girls' lacrosse, the attacker who plays in the center nearest the opponent's goal; first homes are important goalscorers.

Five-Second Rule In girls' lacrosse, a requirement that an offensive player not hold the ball for longer than five seconds if she is closely guarded and the defense is in a position to legally check were checking allowed.

Flag A weighted yellow cloth that an official throws into the air on a penalty that does not stop the action.

Foul Any of a number of illegal actions that can result in a player being penalized, or a team losing possession of the ball.

Foul Out To accumulate five fouls and thus be disqualified from further participation in a game.

Four-Point Rule In some youth leagues, when a team is behind by four or more goals, instead of a face-off after a goal, the trailing team is given possession at midfield.

Free Position In girls' lacrosse, a possession given to the offense when the defense has committed certain fouls; in a direct free position, the player can run, pass, or shoot the ball; if indirect, run or pass.

Goal Both the 6-by-6-foot net, and a scoring shot.

Goal Area In boys' lacrosse, the attack and defensive areas, which are generally restricted to offensive and defensive players.

Goal Circle The circular area, also known as the crease, around the goal, which may not be entered by offensive players.

Goal Line The 6-foot-long line between goal posts.

Goalkeeper The defensive player who blocks shots on goal; also known as the goalie, keep, or keeper.

Green Card In girls' lacrosse, a warning given by an official to a team captain for delay of game.

Ground Ball A ball rolling or bouncing on the ground, which players try to scoop.

Handle The stick part of the crosse; also known as the shaft.

Head The top, roughly triangle-shaped part of the crosse; it is usually plastic and has stringing to hold the ball.

Holding Illegally impeding the movement of another player, such as by grabbing the body or stepping on the crosse.

Intercrosse A type of lacrosse mostly played in Europe that is noncontact and uses a softer ball; also known as soft lacrosse.

Isolation Moving teammates away from the ball carrier so he or she can attempt one-on-one moves against a defender.

Lax A slang term for lacrosse.

Loose Ball When neither team has control of the ball.

Major League Lacrosse The outdoor men's professional league in the U.S.

Man-Down Defense Defensive schemes designed to deal with the other team's one- or more man advantage; akin to a "penalty kill" in ice hockey.

Man-on-Man Defense A defensive tactic in which each defender is assigned to mark a specific offensive player (as opposed to defending an area, as in a zone defense).

Mark Guarding an opponent closely, such as a stick's length.

Mesh The typically nylon stringing that is found in the head of a lacrosse stick.

Middie Back In boys' lacrosse, a call made by a defenseman as he carries the ball over the midfield line on a clear, telling a midfielder to stay on the team's defensive half of the field, to avoid an offsides call.

Midfield Area In boys' lacrosse, roughly the middle third of the field, on each side of the center line.

Midfield Line The line across the center of the field of play; also known as the center line.

Midfielder In boys' lacrosse, the three midfield players who play both offense and defense; also known as a middie.

Modified Pocket A deeper than regulation pocket, up to half a ball below the bottom edge of the sidewall, that some beginning youth leagues allow to be used.

Modified Stick Check Checking a stick if it is below shoulder level, and by using a downward motion away from the other player's body; a rule used in some intermediate-level girls' youth lacrosse leagues.

Moving Pick An illegal pick, because the player setting it is not stationary.

Offside In boys' lacrosse, a penalty situation, in which a team does not have at least four players on the defensive or three players on the offensive side of the midfield line.

On-the-Fly Substitution Player subbing done while play continues on the field.

Outlet Pass The first pass from the goaltender to a teammate that starts the transition from defense to offense.

Overhand The most basic type of pass and shot, by moving the crosse with an over-the-shoulder motion.

Pass Throwing the ball to a teammate.

Penalty Box The area where players who have committed certain types of fouls must go until their penalty time is up and they are allowed to return to the playing field.

Penalty Lane In girls' lacrosse, a path to the goal that is cleared for the attacking team during a free position.

Pick An offensive player without the ball stands still in order to block the path of a defender; youth lacrosse restricts picks, depending upon age and gender.

Pocket The part of the crosse head where the ball is carried and cradled, made of a nylon mesh or a leather and nylon weave.

Point In girls' lacrosse, the defender who plays in the center nearest her team's goal; she marks the other team's first home.

Poke Check A stick check in which a defender uses the head of the stick to stab at the stick of the person with the ball.

Red Card In girls' lacrosse, a disqualification from further play in a game, due to receiving two yellow cards; a red card can also be given for fighting or unsportsmanlike play, in which case the player is also disqualified from the next game.

Release The notification an official gives to a player in the penalty box that he or she may re-enter the game.

Restraining Box In boys' lacrosse, the attack or defensive area.

Restraining Line In girls' lacrosse, a line across the field approximately thirty yards in front of each goal; only seven offensive and eight defensive players (goalie included) may be within the restraining line at any time.

Ride Marking offensive players as they move upfield, in an attempt to prevent them from receiving a pass.

Roll Dodge An offensive move in which a player carrying the ball approaches and then quickly pivots around a defender.

Save A shot on goal that is stopped by a goalie.

Scoop A running pick-up of a ground ball, by bending over and scooping the ball into the head of the stick.

Scoring Play An ongoing opportunity for the offense to shoot the ball into the goal.

Screen An offensive player whose positioning is such that he or she blocks the goaltender's view of a shooter.

Second Home In girls' lacrosse, the attacker who plays in the center of the opponent's half of the field, between first and third home; second homes are often playmakers and accurate shooters.

Shaft The pole part of the lacrosse stick, which traditionally was wood but is now typically metal; also known as the handle.

Shoot Flinging the ball at the net with the intention of scoring.

Sidearm A way of passing or shooting the ball in which the crosse is moved out from the side of the body parallel to the ground, as opposed to the vertical movement of an overhand pass or shot.

Sidelines In boys' lacrosse, the lines that mark the side edges of the field.

Sidewall The two sides of the lacrosse stick head, which define the top of the pocket.

Slashing An illegal contact of the crosse on an opponent's body.

Slide A defender shifting to cover a new opposing player, usually because the player has gotten past a defender and is a threat to score.

Slow Whistle In girls' lacrosse, a raised flag by an official due to a major foul by the defense in the critical scoring area when an attack player is on a scoring play; the fouled player has the choice of continuing play and taking a shot or stopping play and receiving a free position.

Spearing An illegal body check, in which initial contact is made by a player's helmet.

Special Substitution Area Off-field areas where players wait to get into the game.

Sphere In girls' lacrosse, the imaginary 7-inch protective zone around the head; stick checks are not allowed to break this sphere.

Split Dodge An offensive move in which a player carrying the ball in one direction suddenly darts the other way.

Stand In girls' lacrosse, all players except the goalkeeper (if she is inside her goal circle) must come to a complete standstill when an official blows the whistle.

Stick Check Striking the ball carrier's stick with your stick in an effort to dislodge the ball.

Take-Out Check A body check, illegal in youth lacrosse, in which the defensive player lowers his head or shoulder with the force and intent to knock the offensive player onto the ground.

Third Home In girls' lacrosse, the attacker who plays in the center nearest midfield; third homes are key players for making transitions from offense to defense and vice versa.

Third Man Despite the name, this is a position in girls' lacrosse—the defender who plays in the center, marking the other team's third home.

Three-Pass Rule A requirement in some beginning leagues that the offense make at least three passes before shooting.

Three Seconds A violation in girls' lacrosse, in which a defender who is not marking an opponent remains in the eight-meter arc for longer than three seconds.

Throat The part of the crosse head at the top of the shaft.

Unsettled Situation A loose ball or sudden turnover that scrambles defensive positions.

Wall Ball A popular practice method of throwing a ball off of a wall to perfect catching and passing.

Ward An illegal move in which a player with the ball in his stick uses a free hand to push or interfere with a defender's stick.

Wing Area In boys' lacrosse, the midfield area near the sidelines, designated by a line that midfielders must be behind during a face-off.

Yellow Card In girls' lacrosse, a warning given for certain types of major fouls; a player who receives two yellow cards in the same game must sit on the bench for the rest of the game.

X The area directly behind the goal.

Zone A type of defense in which players guard an area rather than specific offensive players.

RESOURCES

US Lacrosse
Youth Council
113 W. University Parkway
Baltimore, MD 21210
Phone: (410) 235-6882
Fax: (410) 366-6735
Internet: www.uslacrosse.org

Canadian Lacrosse Association
2211 Riverside Dr., Suite B-4
Ottawa, ON K1H 7X5
Canada
Phone: (613) 260-2028
Fax: (613) 260-2029
Internet: www.lacrosse.ca

GAMES

ATTACKER
BALL
CARRY
CLEARING
CRADLING

CREASE
DODGE
GOALIE
HELMET
LACROSSE

MARKING
PASS
POCKET
REFEREE
SCOOP

SHOOT
SLASHING
THROW
WHISTLE
WING

```
J  M  P  R  J  W  S  J  N  M  Q  W
J  F  B  V  H  E  C  R  E  A  S  E
V  N  N  H  S  T  O  H  L  O  P  J
L  G  B  I  R  M  O  F  H  H  S  T
V  G  G  W  E  A  P  O  G  U  S  H
P  O  B  W  F  R  R  D  O  K  L  R
O  A  M  J  E  K  U  B  Y  H  A  O
C  L  E  A  R  I  N  G  R  R  S  W
K  I  M  N  E  J  B  W  I  H  H
E  E  C  U  E  G  U  H  W  I  I  K
T  I  O  A  O  T  Y  E  H  L  N  L
A  L  N  C  R  A  D  L  I  N  G  G
K  O  D  J  E  R  R  M  S  Z  R  H
P  J  H  D  K  H  Y  E  T  G  D  O
D  A  F  K  D  O  E  T  L  P  O  C
P  K  S  H  O  O  T  J  E  R  D  J
B  U  Y  S  K  P  K  R  U  H  G  T
A  I  J  T  A  T  T  A  C  K  E  R
L  B  P  L  G  K  I  R  J  F  J  E
L  A  C  R  O  S  S  E  T  D  B  L
```

WORD FIND

CROSSWORD

ACROSS

1 Nickname for lacrosse

4 Box where players who have committed certain types of fouls must go

5 You need to do this to gain possession of a ball on the ground

8 In girls' lacrosse, the defender who marks the other team's first home

11 In boys' lacrosse, the area around the goal the team is shooting at

12 The most basic way to shoot or pass the ball

14 Another name for the shaft part of the crosse

15 A type of dodge often used when running toward a defender

16 A boys' lacrosse team is _ _ _ _ _ _ _ _ if it does not have at least four players on the defensive side of the midfield line

18 A _ _ _ _ whistle is used for a major foul by the defense in the critical scoring area when an attack player is on a scoring play

19 Nickname for a midfielder

20 A shot on goal that hits the ground in front of the goal line

21 An offensive player can set this by standing still in the path of an defender

DOWN

2 The girls' lacrosse field has an 8-meter _ _ _

3 In girls' lacrosse, only seven offensive and eight defensive players may be within this at any time

6 The initial pass from the goalie that starts the transition to offense

7 The type of offense used when the other team has a player in the penalty box

8 A type of stick check

9 The rocking action that keeps the ball from falling out of the pocket

10 A stick in which up to half a ball goes below the bottom edge of the sidewall

13 A body _ _ _ _ _ is very different in boys' and girls' lacrosse

15 An illegal action that leads to a player penalty or to a loss of possession

17 Offensive player positioning that blocks the goaltender's view of the shooter

18 A shot on goal intercepted by the goalie

19 To closely guard an opposing player

ACROSS

1 LAX
4 PENALTY
5 SCOOP
8 POINT
11 ATTACK
12 OVERHAND
14 HANDLE
15 FACE
16 OFFSIDES
18 SLOW
19 MIDDIE
20 BOUNCE
21 PICK

DOWN

2 ARC
3 RESTRAINING LINE
6 OUTLET
7 EXTRA MAN
8 POKE
9 CRADLE
10 MODIFIED POCKET
13 CHECK
15 FOUL
17 SCREEN
18 SAVE
19 MARK

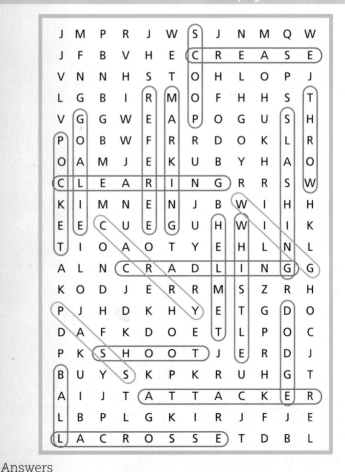